AF439750

Bitter Rants
and
Love Poems

Geoffrey Dicker

This book is a work of fiction. Names, characters, places and incidents are either the product of the author's imagination or are used fictitiously. The reader should consult a medical, health or competent professional before adopting any of the suggestions in this book or drawing inferences from it. The author disclaims all responsibility for any liability, loss or risk, personal or otherwise which is incurred as a consequence, directly or indirectly, of the use and application of any of the contents of this book. Any resemblance to actual events, locales or persons, living or dead is purely coincidental.

Cover art by Geoffrey Dicker

Copyright © 2021 by Geoffrey Dicker
All rights reserved
Including the right of reproduction
In whole or in part in any form.

Manufactured in the United States of America

ISBN-13: 9798451334263

First Edition

Bitter Rants
and
Love Poems

Contents

A Moment of Silence To Remember Those Who Are No Longer With Us ....Page 1

Trigger Warning..Page 2

The Future..Page 4

Profile..Page 6

Hollywood Ending..Page 8

Love Vaccine..Page 10

Not My Department...Page 12

My First Love..Page 14

Silence on a Sunday Morning.................................Page 16

Unrequited Dick Pics..Page 18

This Is Why Rome Burned.....................................Page 20

Proud to be Rich...Page 22

Register Your Complaints......................................Page 24

Social Media Makes Me Wanna Kill Myself...............Page 26

Saturday Morning...Page 28

Blackout Drunk...Page 30

I Think, Therefore I'm Censored........................Page 32

Reevaluate, Recalibrate...................................Page 34

Wrong All Along...Page 36

Thoughts and Prayers......................................Page 38

Twentieth...Page 40

Kiss Ass...Page 42

Cancel Yourself...Page 44

1st Street...Page 46

Texting Idiots...Page 48

We're All a Little Dark......................................Page 50

Politics of Diversion..Page 52

5 Years Since we Said Goodbye........................Page 54

I Understand Why People are Bitter...................Page 56

And They Lived Happily Ever After.....................Page 58

The Sin of Apologizing.....................................Page 60

I Believe In Humanity.......................................Page 62

I Am Not Your Homo...Page 64

Also By Geoffrey Dicker....................................Page 66

Acknowledgements..Page 67

About the Author...Page 68

A Moment of Silence To Remember Those Who Are No Longer With Us

<u>**Trigger Warning**</u>

Emotional support drug

They said it's not addictive

Where is my hug?

Every day gets more constrictive

My phone needs attention

I need an intervention

I keep going online

Wasting more time

Can't tell what's real

I have all the feels

The tide turns

My anger burns

I've been triggered.

Someone asked my thoughts

I said things I should have not

Negativity is coming at me from all sides

The only place I can hide

Is behind my keyboard

Real world overstimulation

Your device wants you to give into temptation

I used to think I was crazy

Wasting time makes me feel lazy

Don't call me a coward

I can't hide my pride

I just happened to be on the right side of the wrong part of

history

I can't tell you why

It's a mystery

I said what I said

Because the thoughts in my head

Needed to escape

They'd been triggered…

<u>**The Future**</u>

The Future

Every mind is graffitied

Space age garbage can

No more Uncle Sam

Tom's still around

They can't seem to bring him down

Seems mixed up

But everyone is distracted

The facts are redacted

Stupid shit exists

Like discrimination of race

When politicians are looking you in the eye

And lying to your face

Wake up or not

Woke is boring

Politically correct whoring

You won't catch me dead without a smile

At the gates of whatever

They are not going to collect our misery

And exchange it for fun

You do you

Don't speak for me

Mind your own business

We all deserve the key

They said we'd learn from history

The facts are pretty obvious but nothing is done

Enjoy the moment

It probably won't last

I'm not so sure the future

Will be any different than the past

Profile

Must love dogs

So I can love you less

Nothing against you

I honestly confess

You will always be number two

Even though I seek the one

Really what I need is a night of fun

Or a vacation from my reality

Everyone is fucked up and they don't even see

But enough about me

Let's talk about you

I have a long list of things I don't want you to do:

Smoke, drink, overthink

Please be rich,

Have a nice dick,

Don't be a prick.

Be kinky or kind

Don't hang around all the time

But when I need you

Please come to my side

Extra-curricular activities don't have to be a part of the ride

Rest assured, I won't judge you

However you decide.

Here's a photo of my friends

That I like better than you

Would be best if you got along with my crew

I'm not giving them up

When you're not going down

And it's rude not to like food

Or watch tv

That's another side of me

I haven't looked in the mirror

Except to see my pretty face

But not the behaviors I probably should replace

<u>Hollywood Ending</u>

If you knew the plot

The hero's journey would be boring

Stay on the path?

You'd say no and just laugh

The discovery is the reward

It's not so pleasant when you find pain

It's not so pleasant when you're broke

It's not so pleasant when your lover leaves you

But maybe life is but a joke

Laugh now

Die later

Cool running

Clocking some miles around the sun

You're boring if you're ever bored

You're not trying hard enough

If you're ever ignored

Wish I knew that at the beginning

It might have prevented pain

Or just delayed it until I rode off into the sunset

Never looking back, feeling no regret

Why be a victim when you can be a victor?

There's never been a better time to gain sympathy

I don't trust you and you don't trust me

Played each other like a game

Neither one of us scored

You refuse to give credit, yet you want the credit

There will be no Hollywood ending

Because you have to give it all back

So you can stop your crying

And go out the way you came in

Naked, alone, afraid and dying

<u>Love Vaccine</u>

Did you ever want it?

Spread from the head to the heart

Baby break it down

The journey of 1000 miles was over

Before the start

Who is the disease and who is the cure?

New directions in sadness

Too close to hear the obvious

Give up the whole thing

Ain't really your thing

We don't exist

There's no reason to resist

No pill can wash it away

The rain comes down

I need a better reason

There's so much choice but I wanted you

Foolish to think you'd feel it too

We are running out of time

Trust is broken

No words are spoken

Our love is infected

It's out of control

We're not at the same place

Close my eyes

Give me a shot

Maybe then I can forget your face

Not My Department

If you want to get from A to B

I'm your man

If you want me to deviate from the original plan

I don't give a damn

I wasn't trained

It's more than my brain can handle

I wasn't always this way

I just have a lot on my mind

War's on the horizon

Everything's going up and nobody is going down

The priorities have shifted

From green to brown

Gaslighting

Infighting

Unsolved mysteries

Love will save the day

I'd like to see proof

I don't believe anything you say

How am I supposed to swipe right

When all my beliefs are on the left?

Sounds extreme

Makes me want to scream

But no one will hear me

Over the sound of all your rules

The truth has been censored

And you call me a fool!

If you unplug

Do you exist?

If everyone is doing it

Why should I resist?

Be a good human

When they take your pic

Don't let them see you're a behind the scenes prick

Does any of this resonate?

If it doesn't, I can't help you

It's not my department

My First Love

You knew enough to be dangerous

Beautiful dragon

Fragile fire

Kept me warm

With your smile

Ice cream eyes

The kind that never lie

Crushing hearts for hobby

Not for sport

I was a challenging stranger

Danced with the devil in heaven

Would have followed you anywhere

You didn't care

Knew I was your slave

Watched you hide the key

Should have known you'd hurt me

I was looking and couldn't see

Wanted to take the shame to my grave

Faced the fact

It was all an act

Walked out on love

Bad vibes only

A pivotal moment in freedom

There's no redemption

Psychopathic ascension

I will encourage and reevaluate

And think of you often

If not for you, my heart would never have grown stronger

I couldn't take it any longer

Thank you for the pain

I knew it was just a game

Everything has healed

Farewell my first love

Silence on a Sunday Morning

The Saturday night violence

Gives way to Sunday morning silence

The service industry sleeps

The day workers creep

If you listen closely, you can hear

The sound that the flowers make

There 's 50 reasons to be blue

Or you can start anew

Wipe the slate clean

Think of more dreams to dream

New heroes will be made

Fallen soldiers will be betrayed

When people don't pause for a moment

Of silence on a Sunday morning

Focused too much on the ending

When the middle is what matters

It's been a long time since things were laid out this way

More reasons to celebrate a new day

Each one is a success

Even if it's not always the best

As people awake

There's more noise

Separate from it

It's your choice

Return to the peace

And silence on a Sunday morning

Unrequited Dick Pics

It's not weird to expose myself to you

I only came here to bare my soul

Get your thoughts

Discover all the things I am not

In the ultimate popularity contest

I only seek your approval

They say I am a big deal over seas

16 straight months

I've never yet missed a royalty

You wanted to see a little more

I want to show you a little less

I captured the moment just for you

A little shameless, I confess

Except I don't

I told you I can't take it

I know you're asking yourself "can't or won't?"

It's close enough so don't you call my bluff

Different cities

Different worlds

I always seem to know when you're coming

You always seem to know when I'm going

Sexual intellectual

You may talk to others

But eventually you return to me

You don't have to tell me you feel it too

I'm not the greatest judge of character

And court is not in session

"Guilty!"

But I set you free

This is Why Rome Burned

Too many people

Too many ideas

Obvious to some

Threatening to others

All these followers and no place to go

There's more than one way to live

Only one way to die

Change the year

You won't change the fear

The mission was to bring people together with division

No one said a word

Living by rules our ancestors made

I don't know about you

But to me it sounds absurd

Who was the expert on right and wrong?

The groove was messed up for your song

You wanted to sing it anyway

And you expected everyone to listen

Wanted a hit

It didn't mean shit

In another generation, you could have struck gold

But you were too busy fighting for likes

Road to nowhere

You've got no one to blame

Except your rigid ways

And your limiting beliefs

Couldn't make you understand why

The world spins around

This is the reason Rome burned down to the ground

<u>**Proud to be Rich**</u>

No apologies will be given

All debts will not be forgiven

I've got some things to say

You will probably not be ok

Zero fucks, awestruck

I'm proud to be rich

I have a nice dick

I use it a lot

I'm catty, I'm a bitch

Sometimes my intentions aren't pure

It's a sickness and there is no cure

I'm selfish both in and out of bed

Love that narcissistic head

I worked I hard for what I have

Never asked anyone for a dime

More concerned with the journey than the climb

I wish I had something more exciting to report

How can I when

My own friends and family rarely offer their support?

Am I supposed to feel guilty because you slept?

Am I supposed to hug you for all the times you wept?

It's not going to happen

Don't have a fit

Newsflash: the world doesn't owe you shit

Wealth does not equal health

Get off your cloud

If you want to be treated special, then act special

Take my privilege, I don't use it

It's just an excuse

Cut me loose

A lot of people I know with money

Are so miserable, they don't find anything funny

You don't need money to be rich

The view from the top doesn't show the game

I won't always be a winner

But you'll never forget my name

This is not a victory, this is not a defeat

Don't call bullshit on me

I kept the receipts

Register Your Complaints

Hatred is lovely

You just need to know where to shop

We're not here to collaborate

We're here to stir the pot

Seems someone has been robbed of their peace

Who is alive and who is deceased?

Exchanged slave paper

Cultural relevance shaper

Register your complaints here

No need for a court of law

When the social media atheists

Decide to find religion

Guilty until proven dead

People discover god in mysterious ways

In the future

Anger will bring people together

No more small talk about the weather

No more communication at all

The more devices, the higher the wall

Togetherness was an illusion

To create obvious confusion

If you can't shout louder

Type prouder

Semi-celebrity brings the pain

Gives everyone another reason to complain

A reckoning is coming

I still believe

Have a seat

Your grievances will be heard

In the order they were received

Social Media Makes Me Want To Kill Myself

Can I get an amen, a comment or a like?

I want to see my traffic spike

In life traffic is bad and here it is good

It's another thing that doesn't make sense

And there's no defense

From when you fall under the spell

Addiction, reality fiction

Hanging with electronics instead of people

Approval from the algorithm

Everyone is a loser in digital prison

Fix me now

Digital buzz

Gives me such a thrill

Some people take pills

I've read about them

The reviews were bad

How could so many people know so little?

Agreement makes people mad

Two levels below

Dumbed down

Popularity is a drug whose high is a low for society

Enjoy the mediocrity

If you seek fame

Soul exchange

Maxed out karma

It's all a game

There's no way out

Love to hate you

Hate to love you

Unplug and you're off the grid

Ultimate freedom or social isolation?

The choice is no longer yours

In hindsight we screwed up

Death is the only exit now

Saturday Morning

You can't win if you don't gamble

Will you take the dare?

Cross the bridge

Defeat the freaks

Who want to see you fail

Don't worry about me

I don't need your prayers

We have different gods

Move on without me

You deserve to be worshipped like Saturday morning

I can't give you more than I already have

If it's not enough

It's tough

Not everyone gets their wishes fulfilled

In this crazy world

If we could meet up for naked pizza again

Sometime in the future

I'd like that

Unless you're full from all the excuses we both made

To make this not happen

It takes two to dance

It takes one to realize a cliched existence

Will kill both parties

You deserve more

Don't be a stranger to these strange times

We'll always have that Saturday morning

Where time stopped

And everything was perfect

Until that afternoon

Blackout Drunk

Hell is just heaven with different lighting

You'd do anything to go

Your friends are saying yes

Your heart is saying no

Wild child

Let out long enough to live up to your name

An evening to remember

A night to regret

Lost control of your soul

Disobeyed alien law

Got off the path

No turning back

The city made me do it

Hooray for Hollywood!

Looking for a way to place the blame

When the blood was spilled in your name

Bad luck legend

Proud to be a fuck up

It's possible to achieve anything

Blue heaven

Stoned prince

Witness a new chapter

Remain the old you

Apology owed and not granted

A happy ending is all but impossible

The golden ticket exchanged for a quick hit

Times is up and you're out of luck

Judgment day arrives when you open your eyes

Afternoon sun feels like a gun to your head

Devastating icon

Soon you will be gone

Burning in your cell

Feeling like hell

Making promises to yourself you know are just junk

Give me sobriety after being blackout drunk

I Think, Therefore I'm Censored

The snoberatti tried to cancel my parade

In the eyes of the world

I was over before I was made

Too bad for me because I was on the verge of getting paid

As a result of all the groundwork I've laid

Angry at me

Focused on the smarter child

Could you ever really love me

When eye cabbage was how you drain your poison

Act as if every blow job could be your last

New thoughts

The captain of the ship

Dropping paper in a post-google depression

Vibes are gone

Down to the felt

I hit the slide

It was darkest before the light broke through the cracks

Why wait to tell your enemy to fuck off?

Sweet poet

Sharp like a rock

Skinny love in brick city

Purple headed words in a landmine

Every new thought

Encyclopedia dramatica

Take away my keyboard and I'd have nothing to say

I wouldn't have said those things to your face anyway

I finally went viral and everyone has been vaccinated

I think, therefore I'm censored

Reevaluate, Recalibrate

I saw it online so I assumed it was true

Shared my past in the present

It's no longer who I represent

I thought I'd dust it off for attention

Of course, I won't mention that

I'm just getting real with myself

Because no one will see it

It's like meditating when you don't need it

Never read the comments

Tragedy strikes

Not enough likes

Change the strategy

Doesn't set me free

I should dump these folks

They really don't care

Only speaking because they are not spoken to

It's the way of the new

I liked it better in the old

Unfortunately I haven't a clue

How to really influence people

Nor do you

But it helps us sleep

Thinking we have power

Instead we've wasted our finest hour

Scroll on by

Until we die

Or we could arrive at something cool

The lost class

Critical mass

Needs a good smack

Reevaluate, recalibrate

When you've done so

Check back

<u>Wrong All Along</u>

What if the government poisoned us?

What if everything we thought was true was a lie?

Would you spit in your hero's eye?

Would you root for all the good guys to die?

How hard would it be to admit

We were wrong all along?

More guns than roses

God and the devil born from the same mama

Disturbing the peace

Causing drama

Stand down

Over analyze

What a world

Graduation day failure

Evil yoga

Thoughts misdirected

Technological slave

Who's going to save you now that your friends have gone?

Drowning

Raise your hand

Heaven is a part of infinity

So is hell

So is the palace where we dwell

The past is not in denial

The present is a gift

Reality is a nightmare

Nightmare is reality

In the end it escalated exponentially

Thought we could get past it

Thought we would outlast it

Non binary

Computer malfunction

50 shades of bitter

Disconnection is the only thing that can save us

And even then...

<u>**Thoughts and Prayers**</u>

People are dumb

They are just looking to be led

Down the drain

It's such a shame

The stairway to heaven

Is located in the basement of hell

Don't ask

I won't tell

It's these same people offering thoughts and prayers

That might drive a body to despair

No guarantee of positive energy

Everyone is out for their self

And they act like when they die

They'll be taking their wealth

I've got some bad news

Some of it might be good

There is no cure

You can't go back

There is no finish line on this infinite track

Don't be angry

Don't be in denial

The truth rarely comes out

Because it does not like being on trial

If you search

You will find

It's easier sometimes to just close your eyes

Blind faith

Mental rape

Let them take control

The train is nearing the edge of the track

If it gets derailed

It's never coming back

<u>**Twentieth**</u>

I gave up on my first dream

Some art school gangster

Gave me bad advice

So I moved on

And my temporary crush found a new forbidden love

With number 2, I didn't have a clue

So on and so forth until I found the silence

All I had to do was walk past the devil

And never look her in the eye

She wants to take what's yours

And give it to some other guy

I've seen it happen before

Lots of other times

1 trick ponies trying to escape from the zoo

15 days later, I had a dream about me and you

It was like the real world except

I only let myself get disappointed

Because I had nothing else to do

I'm stronger now, no thanks to you

I only have myself to blame

If at first you don't succeed in this game

Don't give up when you get to 19

The twentieth time could ignite the flame

<u>**Kiss Ass**</u>

Please don't make me get on my knees

Gas chamber of shame

Close my eyes

Aim high

Feel so low

Change my name

It's not about approval

Inhibition removal

I support you in public

Behind your back I talk shit

This is the way of the world

So cut me some slack

Lift you up so the sun shines on me

Clever as an extinct bee

No one notices because they are doing it too

If you're caught

Play the fool

It's just ice

I'll tell you I love you

Public relations

Private altercations

If people wanted the truth

Things wouldn't be this way

Illusion is what they want

Glitz and glamour

Makes the people clamor

It doesn't matter if your content is good

Either you luck out or get the fuck out

Don't forget that garbage is king

Kiss the ring

You'll ascend

Let's exchange money for soul

This too shall pass

Such is the life for a kiss ass

Cancel Yourself

While you were busy decomposing

I was busy living

Your generation is full of shit

Life is hard

Like my dick

I'm not going to force it on you

So relax you little prick

You expect a hug

And you take all these drugs

And you think we're the ones that are crazy

My generation was not lazy

We made the art you are trying to censor

Jealous because you can't make the grade

Just wait until you get betrayed

Documented living does not make a life

A million pictures about nothing

Not worth a thousand words

How do you expect to bring people together with division?

You're throwing away the key to your own prison

When you're standing at the gates of hell

There will be no one there to tell you you're a winner

Church robes don't excuse the sinners

I'm glad I sinned

It made me win

I did everything with no regrets

If that makes you upset

Don't cancel me

Cancel yourself

1st Street

Meet me on 1st Street

We haven't a second to lose

Live in the now

I'll show you how

Maybe we can be each other's muse

Lower your expectations

Then lower them some more

In a kingdom full of lust

Let's engage in honesty and trust

Midnight romance

We dance the delicate dance

Dreams of happiness

Boulevard of darkness

Silent desires

Undisclosed locations

Where are you on the grid of love

Taken or forsaken?

I offer no guarantees

New text in an old world

I can offer a lot

But I won't give you drama

Mourn it later

Into the light of collaboration we go

Passion tornado

Late night agenda

All requests have been fulfilled

Free yourself to commit

I won't ask a 3rd time

If my feelings were wrong

Let's separate

I wear a crown of shame

There is no one to blame

If you're ever lost or feel unseen

Look me up

I'll be waiting on 1st street

Thinking of all the possibilities that could have been

I won't be there forever

Just until the light turns green

Texting Idiots

The texting idiots are texting idiots

Can't it wait?

It's not like I'm standing at your gate

And monsters are going to eat me alive

If you don't give me attention

But I've failed to mention

There are trolls emerging

My stats are surging

I need to feed the beast

Hold it in for a second at least

Checking in

Checking out

Getting closer to the edge

So much for the pledge

Live in the now and ignore the cultural vow

We should have never let them take control

We let everyone buy our soul

And we sold them too cheap

Now we're in too deep

In a world where everything is worse than the day before

Only a few people have scored

At the expense of the rest of us

Is there a rocket ship to take me away?

I can't face another day

Crap is king

Train wrecks are the new entertainment

Reality is not real

The truth cannot be trusted

Nobody is famous

Because everyone is famous

The cure is the same as it's always been

Just say no

We're All A Little Dark

Being good is bad

Seeing happy people makes me sad

I know you feel it too

I've watched your face come alive

When you heard the news your enemy died

Don't try to lie

I've already seen the inside

The fact is, we're all a little dark

Makes for a better story arc

Because nothing lasts

Humans deny their pasts

I've seen the future

You've been written out

No action is required on your part

Who wouldn't want to die for their art?

Discarded canvas

There's no time to get another

What do you do when you can't trust your own brother?

Maybe he's a little dark too

When the light goes out

Join us

There's nothing to discuss

You're either out or you're in

Do you want to lose or do you want to win?

The answer is obvious

The light escapes

Don't speak

I can taste your lies

They're just like your tears

I'll see you later

It's getting dark

Politics of Diversion

Leave innocent people alone

You're not to be trusted

Whoring your integrity

Hoping karma is not real

Milky chaos

Up to old tricks in the new economy

Video game values

Restless wandering eye

How many people can you fuck over

Before they see the stains in your kimono

There's no one on the streets

Demanding the money be released

Pray for Kool-Aid faith

It's a terrible secret

Rotting like fruit inside your head

Mutual lockdown & a vertical smile

Prevents the truth from breathing fresh air

And each day you lay it down

Another protest warrior is silenced by noise

Fact check?

Censored truth

You can't protest if there is no proof

Rest in power

My delicate flower

French fries and rock and roll

Made you look

What were you talking about?

Exactly.

<u>5 Years Since We Said Goodbye</u>

5 years since we said goodbye

Only a miracle could have changed the end

Into a beginning

There was no chance of making you believe

You licked my doubts

I'll bet you couldn't wait to get out

Freedom is a beautiful thing

Commitment made you leave

Lit the match so there was no way to bring it back

You saw right through my eyes

Smiled as you left

Cause of life

Temporary death

Last coin fished out of the wishing well

Nothing granted

Everything gained

In the dictionary next to the definition of pain

There will be a photo of my regret

Can't fix the mistakes of the old

I'll see you again in dreams

You'll see my face every time an angel falls from grace

5 years since we said goodbye

Hello old friend

I wish I loved you

The way you took me for granted

And They Lived Happily Ever After

It's always been a numbers game

I failed math

It wasn't my path

Said hi to everyone just in case

They all ignored my face

But I knew one day you'd come around

Lured you in with my dry wit

And ability to talk about stupid shit

Trippy

Hippie

So glad you picked me

Tell me all the things you hate

So I can be on my best behavior for our date

I won't promise you love

I won't promise you death

The kingdom is ours

Buy now and they'll throw in the stars

Your life will be incomplete if you don't have me

I want my smile to be the first thing you see

When you put your phone down and open your eyes

I won't ever hurt you by telling you lies

Don't be mad at the truth

I am living proof

Come on, take a chance

I believe in this romance

Say yes to saying no

And they lived happily ever after....

I Understand Why People Are Bitter

Social media is the world's worst slot machine

Lots of information exchanged for

Very little green

Found out that I am annoying

No one wants to hear what I have to say

And I have to live with this info day after day

Racists, cheaters, wife beaters

There's no escape

People you thought were real

Turned out to be fake

Afraid of the future, choking on the past

Not thinking about what is at stake

Short lived success

Nothing ever lasts

Bad guys are in power

Everything sweet has now turned sour

Respect the science

You put the F in spelling

Do it for the global good

That statement is very telling

The game of chasing fame

Has brought down the collective IQ

I haven't a clue what to do, do you?

How are we supposed to come together

When we keep separating ourselves?

Martyrs do it better

I can't take the pressure

I have to give it away for free to get people to see

If we don't make serious changes, this is the way it's going

to be

The poor will stay poor and the elite will continue living a

life of glitter

Makes perfect sense now

I understand why people are bitter

<u>**The Sin of Apologizing**</u>

Post this

Censor that

We can't all be wrong for having a voice

Some get to speak

Not always by choice

What's good for some is deadly for others

Having an opinion

Is killing your mother

First moments in heaven

Last thoughts in hell

I would rather hang out where the sinners dwell

The punishment is unrelenting

The bad guys are unrepenting

Maybe we should reexamine the whole thing

If the tide turns

The morality police will want to talk to you

The top is a lonely place

There's not much to do

Take you down

Shake you down

Did you even mean the things you said?

The only way forward is to stop judging

And start listening

There is truth in all cliches

Rest in power?

I think you need a reality shower

Stand tall

Stand behind your words

You can't be canceled by people who never supported you

in the first place

Get back up and commit more crimes

But don't commit the sin of apologizing

When you're not sorry

I Believe in Humanity

Lead with love

They want us to fail

Meditation is key

To setting yourself free

There's more prisons than playgrounds

Why does that have to be?

Don't be in hell

Be heaven bound

Try something new

Talk to someone who is not like you

Agree to disagree

Take it from me

I was once blind but now I see

The choice is up to you

There's a lot to hate

And even more to love

Anyone who tries to stop it

Is someone you should let go of

Open up if you want to receive

Angels everywhere to help you achieve

Life is a series of bitter rants and love poems

But it doesn't have to be

For I still believe

I believe in humanity

I Am Not Your Homo

How you identify

Is none of my fucking business

You do you

And leave me alone

You might think we're the same

But I am not a clone

Live life to the fullest

Instead of being full of shit

Be a good human

Don't be a dick

Life is full of likes

Don't be full of hates

It's an instant gratification world

So make the people wait

Greatness cannot be rushed

Brotagonist

Just friends

Morning glory

Tells a different story

Six secs

No sex

I can be a lot of things to you

But I am not your homo

My world is pink

So don't you think

I am going to be blue

Sticking around waiting for you

Call me a fool

I follow simple rules:

Don't take more than you give

Please don't judge me

Let me live!

Also by Geoffrey Dicker

Sketches of Verbal Alchemy

Unfinished Lyrics

I Won The Internet! – Daily Wit, Wisdom & Selfies,
According to G

Journal of Grievances

Twisted Tales and Very Short Stories

Goddamned! – A Play

Post Celebrity

Paddling Backwards

The Rise and Fall of Utopia – An Oral History

In Bad Company

Acknowledgements

First and foremost, thanks to everyone who has supported me throughout the years. Your love keeps me going and I am deeply grateful. This book would not have been possible without my admiration for Jim Morrison, who taught me that poetry can be anything you want it to be as long as you commit the words to paper. I would like to thank Bill G., Jeffrey F., RW & AJ for being a huge source of inspiration to me for this project. What started as a group of poems eventually morphed into a social media project whereby, I read a poem a day for an entire month. It was a fun and creative challenge and it took me out of my safety zone, which is always good for the soul.

With all my love,

G xx

About the Author

Geoffrey Dicker is the author of 10 books ranging from abstract poetry ("Sketches of Verbal Alchemy") to novels ("Journal of Grievances," "Paddling Backwards," "Post Celebrity," "In Bad Company"). In between, he's written a play ("Goddamned"), a collection of 200 one-page short stories ("Twisted Tales") as well as humor ("I Won The Internet!"). His 2020 book "The Rise and Fall of Utopia – An Oral History" inspired and released in the middle of a global pandemic is a satire mirroring the Covid-19 virus. Three full length albums of his lyrics have been recorded by singer Jim Emmons and his song "Manhunt," performed by Jeremy Gloff, was featured in the film "Eating Out: The Open Weekend." When Dicker is not writing, he enjoys creating abstract paintings. Geoffrey Dicker has lived in Los Angeles, New York and Chicago.

Follow his adventures on Instagram @according2g

www.ingramcontent.com/pod-product-compliance
Lightning Source LLC
Chambersburg PA
CBHW051346150726
48000CB00003B/1069